A MOTHER'S JOURNEY

(Through the Eyes of a Husband)

Written by

RITESH BHARDWAJ

Clever Fox®
PUBLISHING

Chennai • Bangalore

CLEVER FOX PUBLISHING
Chennai, India

Published by CLEVER FOX PUBLISHING 2025

ISBN: 978-93-6707-478-7

AUTHOR'S NOTE

This is not a manual. This is not a perfect story. This is a real journey of a husband, a father, and a man trying to balance work, dreams, and the arrival of new life.

It is written with honesty — the sleepless nights, the moments of helplessness, the joy, the tears, and the rediscovery of love.

If you are a parent, you may find yourself in these pages. If you are about to become one, may this give you a glimpse for the beautiful chaos ahead. And if you are simply reading, may it remind you to appreciate the unseen sacrifices of every mother & parents around you.

Dedication

To my wife, who carried both life and love within her.

To my son, who gave new meaning to my journey.

And to all mothers and fathers, walking the toughest and most beautiful road together.

GRATITUDE

I owe immense gratitude to my parents, whose love continues to guide me; to my in-laws, who stood like pillars during this journey; to my brother-in-law & friends who stepped in when I was stretched; and to my Trek Leaders from Miles To Trek, to Crew from One More Mile running club, my colleagues & my mentors who understood my changing priorities.

From the mountains and endurance sports, I learned resilience, patience, and persistence — lessons that became my lifeline through fatherhood. The climb is never easy, but step by step, the summit always comes into view.

A NOTE TO THE READER

Parenthood is not a perfect journey — it's a balancing act of love, patience, exhaustion, and joy. There will be sleepless nights, anxious days, and moments when you feel completely lost. But there will also be smiles that heal, tiny hands that anchor you, and milestones that make every struggle worth it.

If there is one thing I've learned, it's this: balance doesn't happen on its own; we create it. We create it when we choose to share responsibilities, when we make time to nurture our health and dreams, and when we hold space for our partner's growth alongside our own.

From the mountains and endurance sports, I have carried one lesson into fatherhood: *no summit is reached in one leap.* It's a slow climb, one step at a time, with stumbles, pauses and persistence. Parenthood is just the same — a test of patience, resilience, and faith.

This book is not just about becoming a father. It is about rediscovering love, learning the strength of the mother, and realizing that the family we build is the most important adventure of all.

As you turn these pages, may you find encouragement for your own journey: to embrace chaos, celebrate the little victories, and honor the love that makes a family whole.

CONTENTS

CHAPTER 1

The Silent Beginning — First Trimester

The night before a great trek always carries a certain restlessness: a mix of anticipation, nerves, and the thrill of the unknown. For me, the Annapurna Base Camp trek in Nepal was supposed to be another test of endurance, another adventure in the mountains I called my playground. But this time, the mountains were not the only challenge awaiting me.

We already knew, before lacing up our boots and setting out for Annapurna, that my wife was expecting. A small line on a test strip had shifted our world in ways that no mountain peak ever had. The morning after we learned the news, we visited Pashupatinath Temple in Kathmandu. Standing before the ancient shrine, I found myself quietly praying not for strength on the trail, but for her, for the little life growing inside her, and for the courage I would need as a husband and father. In that instant, life had whispered its biggest truth: my greatest journey was no longer about chasing summits, but about stepping into love, responsibility, and fatherhood.

Still, we decided to trek. Not out of recklessness, but because the mountains had always been our place of strength, our shared ground. Perhaps, deep down, we both understood that this trek would be more than just a climb—it would be the first step in preparing us for the road ahead. Every trail demanded patience, every breath in the thin air taught resilience, and every step reminded us of the power of walking side by side.

And when we returned from the mountains, life placed its seal on the story—the quiet confirmation that the tiny heartbeat we had hoped for was real. It was no longer just about reaching Annapurna's base camp. The greater expedition had already begun—an expedition with no summit, only a lifelong journey of love, endurance, and shared strength.

Shadows and Light of the First Trimester

The first three months of pregnancy are often spoken of as fragile, mysterious, and unpredictable. As a husband, I began to see changes in my wife almost immediately. She had always been the kind of person who could power through a day without stopping, someone who rarely napped. Yet, during those early weeks, I witnessed her lying down, her eyes heavy, surrendering to fatigue she couldn't fight.

That simple act—her taking an afternoon nap—moved me in ways I didn't expect. For me, it was no longer about just "becoming a father." It was about witnessing the strength of a woman silently carrying life within her while her body demanded rest, food, and care in ways she had never experienced before.

Morning sickness, mood swings, and unpredictable cravings soon became part of our daily rhythm. And as much as she was learning to navigate these changes, I was too. For the first time, I had to put myself in her shoes, and practice empathy instead of logic.

Adjustments and Sacrifices

Pregnancy forced us both to adjust in ways big and small. Suddenly, the things we loved—long drives, spontaneous outings, social gatherings—took a back seat. Even on the trek, I found myself constantly aware of her well-being, ensuring she was comfortable, checking her expressions, matching my pace without complaint.

Back home, food became a big subject. Spicy dinners, late-night snacks, and fast-food outings were replaced with healthier meals. Not because we had to, but because I wanted to. There was a sense of shared sacrifice: giving up certain comforts to create a safer environment for her and the little life growing inside.

Then there were the late-night pharmacy runs, something every husband comes to understand sooner or later. At first, it felt like an inconvenience, but soon I realized it was a privilege—a way to contribute, to be part of a process where so much of the burden rested on her shoulders.

My life had always been about maintaining a **work–life–trek–run balance**, but pregnancy added a whole new dimension to that juggling act. Some days I would come home exhausted, but the sight of her tired face would remind me that my role was no longer just about my career or my ambitions. It was about being present, mentally and emotionally, even when my body was drained.

The Mental Battle

Excitement and fear lived side by side in my heart. On one hand, I was thrilled—thinking about holding the baby, planning family trips, teaching my child to run, trek, and dream. On the other, there was the constant voice of doubt: *Will I be a good father? Will I be able to provide enough? Am I ready for this?*

Finance became one of the first things I started planning. Suddenly, I was looking at expenses differently. Savings, insurance, investments-all of which once felt distant became urgent and personal. It wasn't just about building a future for myself anymore; now it was about building a safe nest for my wife and our child.

I realized that mental strength wasn't about having all the answers. It was about staying steady amidst uncertainty, and being calm in the storm when everything felt overwhelming.

Empathy: The Quiet Teacher

Perhaps the greatest lesson of the first trimester was empathy. For years, I had admired my wife's strength in many forms—her discipline, her independence, her laughter. But pregnancy revealed a side of her that I had never known. The way her body was changing, the way she dealt with discomfort, the way she silently carried both joy and worry—it all taught me something profound.

I began to understand that fatherhood doesn't start with holding the baby in your arms. It starts much earlier—when you learn to see through your wife's eyes, when you recognize her sacrifices, when you accept that her strength comes with moments of vulnerability.

Closing Reflections

The first trimester is often spoken of as a test of survival for the mother. But for a husband, it is equally a test of awareness, patience, and emotional maturity. It is when you first learn to set aside your own needs and tune into hers. It is when the idea of a family stops being a dream and starts becoming a responsibility.

Looking back, I often think about that moment before the Annapurna trek. Life gave me two journeys at the same time—one up the mountains of Nepal, and one into the uncharted territory of fatherhood.

Both demanded resilience, both required sacrifice, and both taught me humility.

The mountains I climbed eventually ended. But the journey that began with those two pink lines will last a lifetime.

CHAPTER 2

Blossoming Hopes — Second Trimester

The second trimester felt like a fresh breath of air after weeks of uncertainty and fatigue. If the first trimester was about survival and adjusting to sudden changes, the second was about slowly embracing the journey with joy and anticipation.

By now, the pregnancy was **visibly showing**, and with it came a new sense of reality. My wife's face carried a glow that I had never known. Her energy slowly began to return, and though not every day was easy, there was an unmistakable spark of excitement in both of us. For me, this was the phase where the dream started to take form, where the word "parenthood" felt less abstract and more alive.

A Growing Connection

One of the most memorable parts of this trimester was the frequent hospital visits. Each appointment was more than just check-ups and reports — it became a source of strength and reassurance. The doctor's calm demeanor and the gentle smile she carried whenever she told us that things were progressing well filled us with confidence. Every visit turned into a small celebration afterward — sometimes a quick panipuri date on the way back, other times a pizza date that felt like a reward for the little victories along the journey. Those smiles and those moments weren't just updates; they were fuel for our spirits, quiet reminders that we were moving forward on the right path.

Then came the first magical moments—the sound of the heartbeat, rhythmic and strong, like a tiny drum announcing a new rhythm in our lives. I remember sitting there, listening, with a mixture of awe and disbelief. It felt surreal, almost spiritual, that life was no longer just ours—it was within us, shaping silently but powerfully.

And then the baby kicks began. The first flutter was almost a whisper, but soon, those little movements became a conversation. For my wife, it was an intimate connection. For me, it was the beginning of fatherhood—my first interaction with the baby, though still unseen.

The Role of Protector

By this time, I could feel my role shifting. I was no longer just a husband—I had naturally become a **protector**. Every decision I made carried a new weight. Whether it was about travel, diet, or even late-night social outings, my priorities had shifted entirely.

My life had always been about maintaining a **work–life–trek–run balance**, but now that balance slowed down. Running miles, chasing treks, or planning long weekends with friends didn't feel as important as making sure she was eating well, resting enough, and not carrying heavy burdens—literal or emotional.

It was no longer about me pushing limits, but about creating a safe boundary for her. And strangely enough, that shift didn't feel like a sacrifice; it felt natural, like stepping into a new version of myself.

Family Excitement

If the first trimester was just between the two of us, the second trimester was when the news started weaving its way into the hearts of those closest to us. The excitement in the family circle was contagious. Parents, siblings, and close friends brought in an energy that made the journey even more special. Every phone call, every blessing, every suggestion about names or baby clothes added another layer of warmth.

This sense of togetherness made us realize that our child wasn't just ours—it was a blessing the entire family was ready to welcome. And with that came a certain responsibility, but also a lot of joy.

Challenges in the Glow

Of course, it wasn't all perfect. Pregnancy glow often walked hand in hand with sudden mood changes, cravings, and occasional frustration. There were days when small things triggered tears or irritation, and as a husband, I had to learn the art of staying calm and patient.

There were nights when she would crave something unusual at odd hours. There were mornings when the smallest change in her routine made her uneasy. At first, I found myself confused, even frustrated, but slowly I began to understand—these weren't mood swings to be judged, they were signals of the incredible transformation her body and mind were undergoing.

This period demanded reassurance, not solutions. I realized my job was not to fix everything but to simply stand by her, listen, and let her know she wasn't alone.

A Planner in the Making

With excitement building, I also began to think like a **planner**. From reading parenting guides to watching videos on baby care, I wanted to prepare myself for what lay ahead. Shopping for tiny clothes, researching cribs and strollers, and discussing financial planning became part of my daily thought process.

Each small step—whether s comparing baby brands or calculating future costs, was more than just preparation. It was a way of showing love, silently telling both my wife and our unborn child that I was ready to give my best.

When the Past Walks Beside You

There was also a quiet fear that stayed with us through this phase. A few years back, my wife had gone through the pain of a miscarriage, and that memory lingered like a shadow. It was the same kind of feeling you get when you didn't summit your peak the last time, and now you're back climbing the same mountain again. Or like being marked DNF in a marathon and then standing once more at the start line of the same race years later. The excitement is there, but so is the fear — of history repeating itself, of not being able to finish what you set out for. Every step forward carried both hope and hesitation, and we learned to embrace that duality together.

Mental Well-being: The Balancing Act

The second trimester taught me that **mental well-being is not just for the mother but for the father as well**. The responsibility was heavy, and the future was uncertain. But I learned that my calmness had a direct impact on her comfort. If I panicked, she felt unsettled. If I stayed positive, she carried that strength with her.

I realized that being strong was less about lifting weights and more about lifting moods—hers, mine, and eventually, our family's.

Closing Reflections

The second trimester was a season of hope—a time when the invisible began to feel real, when the glow outshone the fatigue, and when small kicks carried deep meanings.

For me, it was also the chapter where I stepped fully into the role of a husband-father hybrid. Protector, supporter, planner—all rolled into one.

Every hospital visit, every smile from the doctor, every heartbeat we heard was a reminder that life was growing not just inside my wife but inside our relationship too. The bond between us deepened, and the anticipation of meeting our child filled every corner of our lives.

The mountains I once climbed for thrill and challenge now seemed small compared to the mountain of responsibility I was learning to carry—but this climb was filled with joy, love, and purpose.

CHAPTER 3

The Final Stretch — Third Trimester

The final trimester is often described as the longest wait of a couple's life. The end feels so close, yet every day stretches endlessly. For us, this period was a mix of heightened excitement, deep anxiety, and a new level of respect I developed for my wife.

The wait was at its peak, and so were the movements of the little champ inside her. Every day carried new surprises, new discomforts, and new emotions. I often found myself watching in amazement, realizing just how incredible a woman's body is and how it adapts, and perseveres to nurture new life.

The Strain on Her Body

By this stage, the pregnancy was no longer subtle—it was visible, heavy, and demanding. My wife's feet began to swell, her body felt heavier by the day, and sleep became a luxury she could rarely enjoy. Nights were spent tossing and turning, trying to find a position that brought even a few minutes of comfort.

I remember lying beside her, helpless at times, wishing I could take away her discomfort. I could massage her feet, bring her pillows, or help her adjust the bed, but nothing truly erased the strain she carried. As a husband, that helplessness was the hardest part—knowing the person you love is in pain and realizing all you can offer is support and presence.

The little champ inside her had developed its own rhythm, moving and kicking at odd hours. Sometimes it was joyful, filling us with laughter. Sometimes it came at 2 a.m., adding to her sleeplessness. We would lie awake together, watching her belly shift and ripple. Those moments were surreal—tiny reminders that the wait was worth every sleepless night.

The Emotional Anchor

If the second trimester made me a protector, the third trimester demanded I become an **anchor**. My wife's mood swings were sharper now. Some days she was filled with joy, imagining holding our baby soon. Other days, fear crept in—fear of the unknown, of labor pain, or if everything would go smoothly.

I had no magic words to erase her worries, but I learned that being there was enough. Listening, holding her hand, sitting silently through her tears—those small gestures became my language of love.

As a man, society often teaches us to "fix" problems. But this stage taught me that not every problem needs fixing—some just need companionship. And so, I became her safe space, her calm during the storm.

Preparations in Full Swing

The third trimester also brought a sense of urgency. Suddenly, every day felt like a deadline. Hospital bags were packed and repacked. Baby clothes were washed, folded, and arranged. We checked the route to the hospital more than once, made lists of emergency contacts, and discussed every possible scenario.

Family visits became frequent. Parents and relatives came often, offering advice, blessings, and sometimes endless stories of their own experiences. Their presence added warmth, but it also reminded us of the seriousness of what lay ahead. Everyone was excited, but beneath that excitement was the unspoken prayer for a safe delivery and healthy baby.

Those visits also made me realize that fatherhood is not just about one man's journey—it's about becoming part of a bigger circle, a family united by love and anticipation.

Sacrifices and Shifts

By this time, social life, hobbies, and personal routines had completely taken a back seat. Trekking plans, runs, or even late-night gatherings with friends no longer mattered. My focus was singular— being present for her in every possible way.

There were days when exhaustion hit me hard. Work demanded attention, responsibilities piled up, and my own body craved rest. But the sight of her carrying not just her own weight but the weight of a new life pushed me to go further. If she could endure so much, surely, I could sacrifice my sleep, my routines, and my comfort.

Marriage, I realized, is not about equality in numbers but equality in effort. At that time, her body carried more, so my role was to carry her emotionally; to bear her burdens alongside her.

Mental Strength and the Countdown

The final weeks demanded mental strength like never before. The days were filled with a mix of joy and nervous energy. Every kick was celebrated, every doctor's visit was a sigh of relief, and every passing day brought us closer to the big moment.

I found myself counting days, sometimes even hours. Yet, in between the anxiety, I found pockets of joy—watching her laugh at a silly joke, feeling the baby respond to music, or just sitting quietly, dreaming of the life ahead.

For me, mental strength came from togetherness. The two of us, facing the unknown side by side, became my greatest source of courage. I learned to silence my fears, not because I didn't have them, but because she needed me steady.

Closing Reflections

The third trimester was the **final stretch of the climb**, the point where fatigue is highest but the summit is finally within sight. For my wife, it was a test of her body's resilience. For me, it was a test of my emotional endurance.

I remain in awe of how a woman's body transforms and adapts, carrying not just life but also the unspoken fears and hopes of two people. I remain grateful that even in moments of helplessness, I could offer her strength, presence, and love.

The sleepless nights, the swollen feet, the mood swings—all of it was a prelude to the greatest gift life was about to offer us. And as the countdown ticked on, our hearts beat not just for ourselves but for the little champ who was about to change everything.

The wait was almost over. The biggest chapter was yet to begin. The adventure of parenthood was ready to unfold

CHAPTER 4

The Storm and the Sunrise – Labour and Arrival

The Eve of Labour

The day of labour will forever remain etched in my memory. I still remember how my face must have betrayed my anxiety, because my brother-in-law quietly took me out for an early dinner, hoping to distract me. Yet, no matter how hard I tried, I could not eat even a portion of food. My heart was heavy, my thoughts restless, and every bite felt like a burden. Inside, I already knew that nothing could prepare me for the hours ahead.

Back in the hospital, the sterile smell of antiseptic and the sight of nurses hurrying through corridors only heightened the anticipation. Every second felt stretched, as if time itself was holding its breath. She held my hand with a quiet strength, her eyes telling me she was ready to endure what lay ahead. I, on the other hand, felt anything but ready.

Inside the Labour Room

When the doctor allowed me to be present in the labour room, I thought I would be her anchor, her strength. But the reality was very different. The moment I stepped inside and saw the pain etched across her face; my heart sank. I lasted only a few minutes before the weight of it all became unbearable. I couldn't watch the woman I love go through such unimaginable pain.

In those brief moments, though, something shifted inside me. My respect for her multiplied beyond measure. In fact, my respect for all mothers in the world reached a new level. Until then, motherhood was something I had admired from afar, something I associated with my own mother's sacrifices. But in that room, as I stood helplessly watching my wife summon every ounce of her strength, I understood: I truly understood — the power, the courage, and the silent endurance of women.

The Longest Hours

Those hours of labour felt like the longest of our lives. I paced the corridor, prayed silently, and tried to keep my emotions in check. Every cry, every sound that escaped from behind that door echoed in my chest. I wanted to take away her pain, but all I could do was wait.

Then came that moment — the cry. The cry that split the silence of the night and filled it with life. The first cry of our baby. No words can ever capture what it felt like. It wasn't just relief; it was rebirth. It wasn't just joy; it was a miracle unfolding. Tears streamed down my face before I even realized.

The First Night

The first night with our baby was nothing like the movies show. It wasn't peaceful lullabies or quiet bonding. It was chaos — a beautiful chaos.

We couldn't hold it together. The baby cried endlessly, and we stumbled in confusion, exhaustion, and panic. At one point, I remember walking all around the hospital floor, desperately seeking help from the nurses, not knowing how to soothe this tiny soul who had suddenly turned our world upside down.

That night, we learned the first hard lesson of parenthood: nothing would ever go as planned. And yet, even in that madness, there was love.

The First Five Days

The days that followed blurred into one another. Sleepless nights, endless diaper changes, constant hospital rounds, and the struggle of lactation. Every cry of the baby triggered a new round of anxiety. Every nurse's instruction felt like a survival manual we had to memorize on the spot.

My role shifted fluidly — I was caretaker, messenger, and emotional stabilizer. I ran between my wife, the baby, and our waiting family members. I carried updates, reassurances, and at times, simply exhaustion written all over my face. My body ached, but I knew my role was no longer just about me. It was about protecting this fragile unit we had just created.

Redefining Love

Those days, though brutal, transformed me. Watching her fight through labour, watching her learn to cradle and feed despite her own pain, watching her put our baby first at every moment — it redefined what love meant for me.

My respect for her skyrocketed. I began to see love not as grand gestures or perfect words, but as sleepless nights spent holding a crying baby, as the courage to face pain for someone else's life, and as the willingness to give up comfort without hesitation.

The storm of labour was fierce. But when the sun finally rose — in the form of our baby's tiny cry and tiny hands — it illuminated our lives in ways we never imagined. The journey had just begun, but already, I knew: nothing would ever be the same again.

CHAPTER 5

The Fragile Season — Baby's First 3 Months

Entering the Fragile Season

The first three months after birth are often called the "fourth trimester." It is fragile, unpredictable, and overwhelming. For us, it felt like stepping into a storm we didn't know how to navigate. Days and nights merged into one another, and time revolved around feeding schedules, cries, and diaper changes. Sleep became a luxury, fatigue an everyday companion.

Every small movement of the baby became a signal — sometimes for hunger, sometimes for discomfort, sometimes just for comfort in our arms. We learned quickly that nothing would follow a pattern. And yet, amidst this exhaustion, every moment carried a beauty we had never experienced before.

Recovery and the Power of Family

We chose to stay with family during this season, and that decision became our anchor. My mother-in-law played a central role in my wife's recovery phase. From traditional care practices to ensuring she ate the right meals at the right times, she was the silent force who made sure the mother could heal while the baby thrived.

Our fathers — mine and hers — became our mental support system. Their calm presence, their reassurances, and their wisdom gave me the courage I needed on nights when doubts weighed heavy. My brother-in-law and close friends also stepped in, often in simple but significant ways: running errands, keeping the atmosphere light, making sure we didn't drown in the seriousness of it all. Family and friends together became the biggest support system, and without them, this fragile season would have been far harder.

Redefining Balance

Balancing work-life and baby duties was like walking a tightrope. My professional responsibilities didn't disappear, but they suddenly had to share space with midnight feeds, rocking a crying baby, and being emotionally available for my wife. Some days, I came home drained from work, but the sight of her tired face reminded me that my role was no longer just about my career or ambitions.

It was about being present — mentally, emotionally, and physically — even when my own energy was at its lowest. My life had always been about work-life-trek-run balance, but now even that rhythm became a juggling act. Parenthood demanded a new kind of balance, one where presence mattered more than performance.

The Baby's Touch

Amidst the exhaustion, there were moments that made everything worth it. The first time the baby held my finger with those tiny hands, it felt like the world had stopped. The first eye contact — those curious, innocent eyes staring straight into mine — melted away all the fatigue.

Each milestone, no matter how small, became monumental: a smile, a sound, a stretch. These fleeting moments carried a joy that no achievement in work or life could ever match. It was as if the baby was teaching us that beauty lies in the simplest connections.

Mental Battles

But alongside the joy, there were battles within me. Questions about career, responsibility, and identity surfaced often. Was I giving enough to my profession? Was I being the husband my wife needed and the father my child deserved? The weight of responsibility felt heavier than ever before.

Personal time disappeared. Hobbies faded. Social circles became distant memories. Yet, somewhere in that sacrifice, I began to discover resilience. I realized that these months weren't about what I lost — they were about what I was learning to gain: patience, humility, and gratitude.

Gratitude and Strength

Looking back, I see this fragile season as a test of strength — not individual strength, but collective strength. My wife's courage in recovering while nurturing. My mother-in-law's dedication. The quiet but powerful mental support from both fathers. The helping hands of friends and my brother-in-law, who kept things under control.

This wasn't just about us as parents. It was about the ecosystem of love, care, and support that carried us through. It reminded me that while parenthood demands sacrifice, it also deepens bonds, widens perspectives, and teaches us that strength is not about standing tall alone — it is about leaning on each other when the nights are long and the days are heavy.

In many ways, this season reminded me of what I've learned from the mountains and endurance sports. Trekking has always taught me that no summit is conquered alone; it takes teamwork, patience, and the humility to accept help. Running long distances taught me to embrace pain as part of the journey, not as a setback. Parenthood, especially in these first three months, felt like a blend of both — a marathon that tested our endurance, and a climb that demanded resilience and support from those around us.

The fragile season tested us, but it also shaped us. And slowly, with each passing day, we found our rhythm in the chaos.

CHAPTER 6

Growing Bonds — Baby from 3 to 9 Months

Little Movements, Big Milestones

The three-to-nine-month window brought magic into our lives in ways we couldn't have imagined. Suddenly, our son was no longer just a fragile newborn; he was becoming curious, active, and responsive. His first roll on the floor felt like a victory equal to scaling a summit. The day he crawled across the room, chasing after a toy, our laughter filled the air like music.

Every milestone carried its own rhythm. A smile in response to our voices. The first time he recognized his name. The excitement of hearing him babble — small sounds, but enormous in meaning. Each moment reminded me that growth, though gradual, is powerful and unstoppable.

Her Glow Returning

During this phase, I saw my wife regaining her confidence and her health. The body that had endured so much was slowly healing, and with it came a spark of energy. She began laughing more often, moving with greater ease, and enjoying small pockets of "herself" again.

Pregnancy and childbirth had transformed her, but now I could see a balance returning. And with that balance, our bond grew stronger. I understood more deeply that my role wasn't just to be a father to my son — it was also to continue being a partner to my wife. Supporting her recovery was as important as caring for our child.

Shared Responsibilities, New Discoveries

This was also the phase where responsibilities expanded. Introducing solid foods was a learning curve — messy but joyful. Some meals ended up on the floor, some on his clothes, and only a little in his mouth. But each spoonful was a step into the world of growth and discovery.

Doctor visits for vaccinations became regular checkpoints. Baby-proofing the house became a weekend project — every sharp edge covered, every electrical outlet closed, every fragile item removed. Our home began to look less like an adult space and more like a playground designed to protect the little explorer.

Fears and Sleepless Nights

With growth also came new fears. The first cold, the first fever — they shook us in ways that no trek or marathon ever had. We stayed up entire nights, watching his breathing, checking his temperature, waiting for his little body to fight through the illness.

Teething nights were equally brutal. The crying, the sleeplessness, the helplessness — it tested our patience. Yet, in those moments of exhaustion, we found strength in each other. Parenthood was no longer about dividing roles; it was about standing side by side, surviving each night together.

Back to Where It Began

Just after we crossed the three-month mark of our son's arrival, life called me back to the mountains. I was scheduled to lead a group to Annapurna Base Camp. It wasn't an easy decision. Even today, I don't know if it was the right time to leave home, especially after everything we had endured over the last twelve months—the fears, the sleepless nights, the cautious hopes. But my heart said yes.

It wasn't just another trek for me. It was the same trail, the same mountain, where we had first discovered that life had chosen us to be parents. Annapurna was no longer just a peak, but it had become a witness, a companion in this story of ours. Returning there felt less like a professional commitment and more like a pilgrimage. I wanted to bow my head, to whisper my gratitude to the mountain that had silently stood guard at the beginning of this journey.

On the way back, I made sure to visit Pashupatinath Temple in Kathmandu. Standing before the ancient shrine, with the chants and the smoke of incense filling the air, I felt a calmness I hadn't known in months. It was as if the temple and the mountain both reminded me of the same truth—life is fragile, sacred, and far greater than our own understanding.

But perhaps the deepest respect I carried was not for the mountain or the temple—it was for my wife. While I was out there guiding a group through snow and stone, she was guiding our little one through the early rhythms of life at home. I thought about the strength it must have taken for her to manage, the patience, the courage, the endless giving. And in that realization, I knew: every summit I climbed would always belong to her as much as to me.

Finding Our Rhythm, Expanding Our World

Around this time, we also began to rediscover ourselves. I took my wife for a small hike nearby Bangalore, leaving our son with his grandparents. It felt strange to step out without him, but it was also liberating. For a few hours, we were just us again — walking, laughing, sharing silence. That small hike was more than a physical journey; it was a reminder that our relationship mattered, too.

When our son turned eight months old, we chose to travel with him for the first time — from Bangalore to Goa. It was another learning experience — packing endless supplies, dealing with his moods in a new environment, and figuring out how to manage our own anxieties. Travel, once spontaneous, had now become carefully orchestrated. But seeing the world through his eyes — the sound of the sea, the newness of every sight, the way strangers smiled at him — filled us with a different kind of joy. Goa wasn't just a destination; it was the beginning of our adventures as a family of three.

Guilt, Gratitude, and Growing Bonds

For me, the hardest emotional struggle during this phase was the guilt of missing certain milestones because of work — and once, because of a ten-day Himalayan trek. There were evenings when I returned home late only to hear, *"He crawled today,"* or *"He laughed out loud for the first time."* Those words were bittersweet; they filled me with pride yet stung with the realization that I wasn't there to witness them firsthand. Each missed moment left a small ache, a reminder that while I was striving to balance responsibilities, time with my son was something I could never reclaim.

But I also learned to treasure every smile I did witness, every small milestone I could hold in my heart. Parenthood taught me that while

I couldn't be present for everything, what mattered was the depth of presence when I was there.

Our home, once a place to rest between treks, runs, and work, now became the center of our universe. The laughter of our son, the bond with my wife, the support of our family — this was the new world, and it was more fulfilling than anything else I had ever known.

The bonds we built during these months were not just between parent and child, but between all of us as a family. They were growing bonds — fragile at times, demanding always, but endlessly rewarding.

CHAPTER 7

The Little Explorer — 9 to 12 Months

Steps Into a New World

By the ninth month, our son had transformed from a tiny bundle into a curious little explorer. His first steps — wobbly, uncertain, but determined — felt like the opening of a new chapter. Every corner of the house became a mountain for him to climb, every drawer a mystery, every object something to test with his little hands.

The sound of his babbling filled our days, a language only he understood, yet one that connected us deeply. "Da-da," "Ma-ma," and other little syllables weren't just sounds; they were proof that he was slowly weaving himself into our world, and in turn, making his world ours.

A Stronger Mother

I watched my wife evolve during these months. From the fragile recovery phase to now, she had grown into a stronger, more confident woman. She no longer moved cautiously, but with a renewed sense of energy and purpose. Her days revolved around guiding our son, protecting him from falls, feeding him, and laughing at his little discoveries.

Her resilience amazed me. She had endured sleepless nights, countless sacrifices, and the heavy emotional load of being a new mother — yet she stood taller than ever before. The woman I once knew as my wife had now become the pillar of strength in our family.

Our Marriage Redefined

Romance took a quieter, subtler form in these months. There were fewer candlelight dinners or long conversations, but more teamwork, partnership, and unspoken understanding. We weren't always husband and wife in the traditional sense — we were primarily co-parents, allies navigating the daily adventures of raising our son.

There were moments when I missed the "us" we used to be, but at the same time, I realized that this partnership was deeper and more meaningful. Love had changed its expression — it wasn't in grand gestures, but in the way we shared responsibilities, encouraged each other, and stood united even on the most exhausting days.

A World Surrounded by Him

Our lives, once filled with treks, runs, social gatherings, and hobbies, now revolved entirely around our son. His schedule dictated ours. His laughter became our music, his cries our alarm, his tiny victories our celebrations. The world outside seemed distant, almost unnecessary, because our entire focus had shifted inward — into the little world that fit within our home.

I found myself planning weekends not around trails or events, but around playtime, nap schedules, and family walks. Even conversations with friends somehow circled back to him. It wasn't a loss; it was simply a new reality, one where joy was measured in giggles, first steps, and bedtime cuddles.

Endurance and Patience

By the twelfth month, we had lived through a year of sleepless nights, sacrifices, and constant adjustments. There were times I thought I had reached the limits of my patience, only to realize that parenthood continuously demands more — more presence, more calm, more endurance.

The endurance reminded me of the long runs I had trained for and the treks I had finished. Only this time, the finish line wasn't a medal or a summit — it was the smile on our son, the quiet moment of peace when my wife rested, and the deep sense of pride in surviving each unpredictable night together. Parenthood became its own endurance sport — one that tested body, mind, and heart .

Blossoming Gratitude

Looking back on these months, gratitude is the only word that fits. Gratitude for my wife's unwavering strength, for our families who stood by us, and most of all, for the little boy who redefined our lives.

Yes, there was chaos. Yes, there were days when we were drained, irritable, or overwhelmed. But amidst that chaos, our family blossomed. We found joy in simplicity, love in patience, and purpose in togetherness.

As our son turned one, I realized the first year wasn't just about his growth — it was about ours, too. We had grown as parents, as individuals, and as a family. The world may have become smaller, revolving around a little boy, but in truth, it had also become infinitely richer.

CHAPTER 8

Beyond the First Year — A New Chapter

A Celebration and a Pause

When our son turned one, the celebration was more than just a birthday. It was a marker of survival, growth, and resilience — for him, for my wife, and for me. Looking back on that rollercoaster of a year, I couldn't help but feel awe and gratitude at how far we had come.

The tiny newborn we had once cradled was now a little explorer with a smile that could brighten any room, his smile could light up any space. But beyond his milestones, I found myself reflecting on the unseen victories — my wife's strength and patience, our family's sacrifices, and the endurance it took for me to grow into the role of a father.

Pride and Admiration

As I stood by my wife during those early birthday moments, I realized how much respect I had grown for her. Watching her transform from a new mother to a strong, confident parent was humbling. She had carried not just the physical weight of pregnancy, but also the emotional weight of the first year — sleepless nights, endless feedings, and countless adjustments.

Her resilience reminded me of the mountains I had trekked and the long runs I had endured. But this time, the summit wasn't a personal achievement; it was a triumph for all three of us.

The First Family Trek

Not long after his first birthday, we decided to take our son on his first trek — to **Nandi Hills**. It wasn't the toughest climb I had done, but it was one of the most meaningful. Carrying him part of the way, adjusting my pace to his needs, and ensuring his safety at every step tested my endurance in ways I hadn't expected.

The trek wasn't about reaching the top quickly — it was about experiencing the journey together as a family. Watching his curious eyes take in the trees, the breeze, the open sky — it felt like showing him to the world I had always loved. That day, I realized that my adventures would never again be just mine. They would be shared, slower, sometimes harder, yet infinitely more rewarding.

Rebalancing Life and Marriage

Slowly, we found ourselves returning to a rhythm — a life that was more balanced, even if it looked different from before. We built routines that gave space for both our individuality and our togetherness.

Three days a week, my wife chose her walks and runs, reclaiming her strength and independence. Three days a week, I returned to my marathon training with my team, reconnecting with my passion for endurance. On the other days, I adjusted my training to evenings or later hours, so that we could share mornings as a family.

And one day a week, without fail, we walked together as a family of three. That family walk became a ritual, a reminder that no matter how busy or demanding life became, our bond as a family was our anchor.

Rediscovering "Us"

In between parenting and routines, we also began to rediscover ourselves as a couple. Romance wasn't about grand gestures anymore — it was in small acts of care, shared laughter, and the quiet moments we reclaimed after our son fell asleep.

We learned that marriage after parenthood required conscious effort: carving out time for conversation, supporting each other's ambitions, and nurturing our shared vision for the future. Slowly, balance returned not just to our lives, but also to our relationship.

Lessons and Transformation

In the beginning, I was curious; anxious — about what fatherhood would demand of me. Would I lose myself? Would I have to give up the life I loved? Two years into the journey, I have my answer. Parenthood didn't take anything away; it simply reshaped everything.

The treks, the runs, the long workdays — still exist. But they now coexist with bedtime stories, family walks, and baby laughter. My world is richer, fuller, and more meaningful.

Most importantly, I have rediscovered the respect for a mother. Watching my wife's journey has been my greatest teacher. Her sacrifices, her patience, her strength — have taught me that true endurance is measured not in miles run or mountains climbed, but in love given, day after day.

The Lifelong Journey

As I look ahead, I realize parenthood isn't a phase; it's a lifelong journey. It is not about perfection, but about presence. Not about control, but about adaptation.

I started this journey as a husband, a partner in life. Today, I stand as a father — a protector, an anchor, and a man who has learned that the greatest adventure isn't on distant mountains, but right here at home, in the everyday moments with my wife and son.

From the Himalayas to the Western Ghats, the mountains have been my teachers. Every climb carries its own rhythm: some stretches demand patience, others demand strength, and some simply ask that you keep moving, one step at a time. Parenthood is no different. Like a long ascent, there are steep climbs and gentle slopes, moments of exhaustion and bursts of joy. What matters is not the speed, but the endurance and the spirit with which you walk together.

Now the joy is different. Our son walks on his own, cycles around with fearless curiosity, and keeps us on our toes with his endless questions. The responsibilities have grown too — helping him stay safe, watching over him constantly, and guiding him without holding him back. Just like in the mountains, where every stumble is a teacher, here too, every fall becomes a lesson, every smile a summit.

And through it all, the mother — my wife — has been the truest climber of them all. Her body bore the storms, her spirit carried the weight, and her love became the rope that held us together. If I am the anchor, she is the mountain itself — steady, resilient, and endlessly giving. I've come to realize that no endurance sport, no trek, no marathon, compares to the endurance of a mother.

This is not the end of a chapter — it is the beginning of many more. Parenthood is the longest expedition of my life, and just like the trails I've walked in the Himalayas and the Western Ghats, it is filled with beauty, challenge, sacrifice, and wonder. The difference is, this time, I'm not climbing for myself. I'm climbing for us — for my family, for our shared future, and for the love that keeps growing with every step forward.

Some summits are scaled, but the greatest ones are nurtured —
a family, a child, a love that grows forever.